PBR

A Pillar Box Red Publication

in association with

MATCH!
THE BEST FOOTBALL MAGAZINE!

ISBN: 978-1-912456-26-0

Photographs: © Getty Images.

MATCH!
THE BEST FOOTBALL MAGAZINE!

GOAL MACHINES 2020

Written by Jamie Evans

Edited by Stephen Fishlock

Designed by Darryl Tooth

THE COUNTDOWN BEGINS 8

Sebastien Haller
100 Club: West Ham DOB: 22/6/94
Country: France

Riyad Mahrez
99 Club: Man. City DOB: 21/2/91
Country: Algeria

Maxi Gomez
96 Club: Valencia DOB: 14/8/96
Country: Uruguay

Angel Di Maria
95 Club: PSG DOB: 14/2/88
Country: Argentina

Robert Skov
98 Club: Hoffenheim DOB: 20/5/96
Country: Denmark

Troy Deeney
97 Club: Watford DOB: 29/6/88
Country: England

Hakim Ziyech
94 Club: Ajax DOB: 19/3/93
Country: Morocco

STAT ATTACK!
LEGENDARY GOAL MACHINES

511 The only English player to score over 500 career goals is Tottenham legend Jimmy Greaves! He's also hit more league goals in England than anyone else, with 357 net-busters!

60 The most goals ever scored in an English league season was by Everton legend Dixie Dean in 1927-28!

767 Although he claims to have hit over 1,000 goals, officially Brazil legend Pele scored 767 net-busters in just 831 games – what a record!

550 Greaves couldn't match the all-time British record, though – that was set by Scotland and Celtic hero Jimmy McGrory in the 1920s and '30s!

9 At last summer's Under-20 World Cup, Norway striker Erling Braut Haaland scored nine goals in a 12-0 victory over Honduras. Wowzers!

68 Footy legend Gerd Muller has a quality goals-to-game record – his 68 international goals came in just 62 caps for West Germany!

746 Ferenc Puskas has a stunning record of scoring 746 goals in just 754 matches for Hungary, Honved and Real Madrid. He's also the only player to score four goals in a European Cup final!

145

805 According to research, the most prolific player ever is Austrian-Czechoslovakian striker Josef Bican, who scored 805 senior goals!

LEGENDS STAT ATTACK 14

QUIZ 1

WORDSEARCH
Find the Prem's all-time top 30 goalscorers in this mega grid!

FOOTY MIS-MATCH
Take a look at these pics of Kylian Mbappe busting net, then spot the ten differences!

Adebayor	Defoe	Giggs	Lampard	Shearer
	Fireha	Hasselbaink	Le Tissier	Sheringham

EPIC QUIZZES 28 & 48

8 Goal Machines 100-94

10 Goal Machines 93-87

12 Goal Machines 86-81

14 Legendary Goal Machines Stat Attack

16 Goal Machines 80-75

18 Goal Machines 74-68

20 Europe's Big Five Leagues Stat Attack

22 Goal Machines 67-62

24 Goal Machines 61-54

EURO LEAGUES STAT ATTACK 20

26 Goal Machines 53-47

28 Quiz 1

30 Goal Machines 46-41

32 Goal Machines 40-34

34 Europa & Champions League Stat Attack

36 Goal Machines 33-27

38 Goal Machines 26-21

40 Goal Machines 20-16

42 Euros Stat Attack

44 Goal Machines 15-11

DRAW YOUR FAVE GOAL KING 58

46 Goal Machines 10-6

48 Quiz 2

50 Goal Machines 5-4

52 Goal Machines 3-2

54 Goal Machine No.1

56 Goal Machine No.1 Stat Attack

58 Draw Your Fave Goal Machine

60 Quiz Answers

61 Subscribe to MATCH

EUROS STAT ATTACK 42

Sebastien Haller

100

Club: *West Ham* **DOB:** *22/6/94*

Country: *France*

The ex-France U21 forward scored 45 goals in three years at Utrecht, then formed one of the most dangerous attacks in Europe at Frankfurt alongside Luka Jovic and Ante Rebic! That led to West Ham splashing out a club record £45 million on him last summer. No pressure!

Riyad Mahrez

99

Club: *Man. City* **DOB:** *21/2/91*

Country: *Algeria*

Mahrez has scored some of the Prem's most important goals in the last few years. He bagged 17 times in Leicester's amazing title win of 2015-16 then, in his first season at City, helped seal the Prem title with a stunning goal at Brighton on the last day of the season!

Robert Skov

98

Club: *Hoffenheim* **DOB:** *20/5/96*

Country: *Denmark*

Winger Skov has shown some serious goalscoring potential in his career so far. Not only did he bag 29 goals in the Danish League in 2018-19, he was also a superstar for Denmark's U21 squad in qualifying for last summer's Euros, bagging eight goals in ten games!

Troy Deeney

97

Club: *Watford* **DOB:** *29/6/88*

Country: *England*

Watford's all-time top Premier League scorer has a habit of scoring big goals in big games. In 2019, Troy helped fire his side to their first FA Cup final in 34 years, and you won't see a more dramatic strike than his winner against Leicester in the 2013 EFL play-offs!

Maxi Gomez

96

Club: *Valencia* **DOB:** *14/8/96*

Country: *Uruguay*

Uruguay have produced some world-class goalscorers over the years and Gomez could be the latest one. With 31 goals in his first two La Liga seasons, he's scored more league goals than Edinson Cavani had at the same stage of his career – and he won't slow down in 2020!

Angel Di Maria

95

Club: *PSG* **DOB:** *14/2/88*

Country: *Argentina*

Di Maria is better known for his dribbling and sweet left foot than his goalscoring ability, but the winger has bagged double figures in three out of four Ligue 1 seasons. He showed his class in PSG's 3-1 win over fierce rivals Marseille in March with two stunning goals!

Hakim Ziyech

94

Club: *Ajax* **DOB:** *19/3/93*

Country: *Morocco*

During his time with Twente, Heerenveen and Ajax, Ziyech has always been a star of the Eredivisie, but 2018-19 was his best goalscoring season. Not only did he bag 16 league goals, he also hit five in the Champions League – only six stars scored more than that!

Leroy Sane

93

Club: *Man. City* **DOB:** *11/1/96*
Country: *Germany*

2018-19 was the best scoring season of Sane's career, even though he played fewer games than the year before! The pick of his 16 goals in all comps was the quality free-kick he struck against former club Schalke – and there's loads more to come from the rapid young winger!

Bradley Wright-Phillips

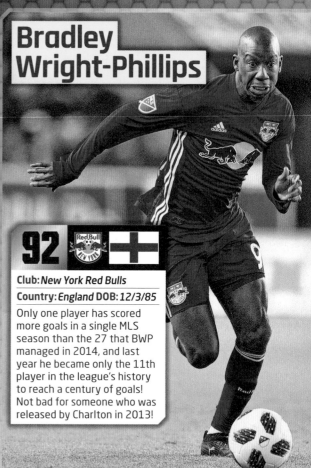

92

Club: *New York Red Bulls*
Country: *England* **DOB:** *12/3/85*

Only one player has scored more goals in a single MLS season than the 27 that BWP managed in 2014, and last year he became only the 11th player in the league's history to reach a century of goals! Not bad for someone who was released by Charlton in 2013!

Ashley Barnes

91

Club: *Burnley* **DOB:** *30/10/89*
Country: *England*

Ex-Austria youth international Barnes has been a consistent goalscorer for The Clarets over the past few years, bagging a career best 12 Prem strikes in 2018-19! He started 2019-20 on fire too, which led to calls for him to be named in Gareth Southgate's England squad!

Aritz Aduriz

90

Club: *Athletic Bilbao*
Country: *Spain* **DOB:** *11/2/81*

Aduriz just gets better with age! He's had three spells with Athletic, but his latest one has been by far the most prolific. Lionel Messi is the only current player with more La Liga goals to his name, while only one star has scored more for Bilbao – club legend Telmo Zarra!

Dele Alli

89 Tottenham Hotspur | England

Club: *Tottenham* **DOB:** *11/4/96*
Country: *England*

Dele bases his game on Three Lions legends Steven Gerrard and Frank Lampard, so he sets his sights on scoring 20 goals a season. He's already got over 40 Prem goals - more than both his heroes at the same age - and could easily match their overall tallies of over 100!

Wilfried Zaha

88 C. Palace | Cote d'Ivoire

Club: *C. Palace* **DOB:** *10/11/92*
Country: *Cote d'Ivoire*

Zaha struck double figures in the Prem for the first time in his career in 2018-19, and he doesn't look like slowing down! The mega skilful winger is so dangerous because he creates goals out of nothing by busting out flash tricks and burning past defenders!

Alvaro Morata

87 Atletico Madrid | Spain

Club: *Atletico Madrid*
Country: *Spain* **DOB:** *23/10/92*

Morata's packed a lot into his career so far, having won trophies and scored goals in La Liga, Serie A and the Premier League, along with starring at a European Championship for Spain! His movement and work-rate make him a top striker - and a brilliant team-mate!

Kai Havertz

86

Club: *Bayer Leverkusen*

Country: *Germany* **DOB:** *11/6/99*

No teenager has ever scored more Bundesliga goals than the 17 Havertz got in 2018-19, and he's one of his country's most exciting young talents. With two really strong feet and insane technical ability, he's likely to be a proper goal machine for years to come!

Mario Balotelli

84

Club: *Brescia* **DOB:** *12/8/90*

Country: *Italy*

After struggling to settle in England, Mario finally found a home in French footy, scoring over 50 goals in just three years with Nice and Marseille! That led to the mercurial talent getting a recall to the Italy squad and a return to hometown club Brescia!

Bruno Fernandes

85

Club: *Sporting* **DOB:** *8/9/94*

Country: *Portugal*

Fernandes was one of the most dangerous midfielders in Europe in 2018-19 with 20 league goals and 13 assists! The highlight of his season was an epic free-kick v Benfica in the cup, but most of his goals came from ace dribbles and runs into the penalty area!

David Villa

83

Club: *Vissel Kobe* **DOB:** *3/12/81*

Country: *Spain*

There aren't many players who've scored goals in four different continents, but Villa's bagged in Europe, Australia, North America and Asia! Spain's all-time top scorer has had a career packed with trophies and will be remembered as a legendary goal machine!

Salomon Rondon

82

Club: *Dalian Yifang* **DOB:** *16/9/89*
Country: *Venezuela*

When it comes to leading an attack as a lone striker, Rondon is one of the best in the world. His ability to scrap it out with defenders is what makes him such a potent goal threat, and he became his nation's all-time top scorer in 2019 with 24 goals for Venezuela. Ledge!

Cristhian Stuani

81

Club: *Girona* **DOB:** *12/10/86*
Country: *Uruguay*

Middlesbrough supporters will remember Stuani as the man who only scored four goals for them in the Prem, but he's been a massive hit since joining Girona. In his first two seasons, only three forwards scored more La Liga goals than the awesome Uruguay striker!

STAT ATTACK!

60

The most goals ever scored in an English league season was by Everton legend Dixie Dean in 1927-28!

767

Although he claims to have hit over 1,000 goals, officially Brazil legend Pele scored 767 net-busters in just 831 games – what a record!

9

At last summer's Under-20 World Cup, Norway striker Erling Braut Haaland scored nine goals in a 12-0 victory over Honduras. Wowzers!

68

Footy legend Gerd Muller has a quality goals-to-game record – his 68 international goals came in just 62 caps for West Germany!

13

The most goals scored by a single player in an international game is 13 – Australia's Archie Thompson achieved the feat in a 31-0 win over American Samoa in 2001!

109

Iran legend Ali Daei is the only player in history to score over 100 international goals!

511
The only English player to score over 500 career goals is Tottenham legend Jimmy Greaves! He's also hit more league goals in England than anyone else, with 357 net-busters!

550
Greaves couldn't match the all-time British record, though – that was set by Scotland and Celtic hero Jimmy McGrory in the 1920s and '30s!

746
Ferenc Puskas has a stunning record of scoring 746 goals in just 754 matches for Hungary, Honved and Real Madrid. He's also the only player to score four goals in a European Cup final!

145
Another Brazilian superstar, Ronaldo, scored 145 goals in just 153 games for Cruzeiro, PSV and Barcelona – before he'd even turned 21!

805
According to research, the most prolific player ever is Austrian-Czechoslovakian striker Josef Bican, who scored 805 senior goals!

Aleksandar Mitrovic

80

Club: *Fulham* **DOB:** *16/9/94*
Country: *Serbia*

Mitrovic arrived on English soil as a raw striker who'd scored 36 goals in just two seasons at Anderlecht, but it took a loan move to Fulham to find his feet. The Serbian hit 12 goals to fire them to promotion from the Championship, and then got another 11 in the Prem!

Everton Soares

79

Club: *Gremio* **DOB:** *22/3/96*
Country: *Brazil*

Not many people had heard of Everton Soares before the summer of 2019 but, after firing Brazil to Copa America glory and winning the Golden Boot in the process, he's now a legend in his home country! Gremio are expecting loads of interest in their star man now!

Anthony Martial

78

Club: *Man. United* **DOB:** *5/12/95*
Country: *France*

Speed machine Martial made an instant impact after joining Man. United in 2015, scoring in a 3-1 win against their biggest rivals Liverpool. Nobody has scored more goals for The Red Devils since then, and we think the best is still yet to come for the colossal young talent!

Josh King

77

Club: *Bournemouth*
Country: *Norway* **DOB:** *15/1/92*

The ex-Man. United trainee struggled at Preston, Hull, Borussia Monchengladbach and Blackburn, but he's been a goal king for Bournemouth. Nobody's scored more Prem goals for The Cherries, and no current player has more goals for Norway either!

Ayoze Perez

76

Club: *Leicester* **DOB:** *29/7/93*

Country: *Spain*

Perez turned down Barça and Real Madrid to join Newcastle in 2014, and 2018-19 was his best season for the club. He scored eight goals in his last nine league games to fire The Magpies to safety, which led to a huge £30 million move to Prem rivals Leicester!

Tammy Abraham

75

Club: *Chelsea* **DOB:** *2/10/97*

Country: *England*

Tammy took the EFL by storm in two different seasons, first netting 23 goals for Bristol City in 2016-17, then firing Aston Villa to promotion in 2018-19! He's got the poaching instincts of a much more experienced striker, and now he's showing it off at boyhood club Chelsea!

Gylfi Sigurdsson

74

Club: *Everton* **DOB:** *8/9/89*

Country: *Iceland*

Sigurdsson's much more than a great goalscorer, he scores great goals! He delivers wicked strikes in big moments – his first touch for Hoffenheim was a stunning free-kick, his first goal for Everton was a 40-yard lob and he bagged Iceland's first ever World Cup goal too!

Glenn Murray

73

Club: *Brighton* **DOB:** *25/9/83*

Country: *England*

Murray is a rare thing in footy – a hero to both Crystal Palace and Brighton fans! His goals fired The Eagles to the Prem in 2012-13, and then he did the same for The Seagulls four years later! He's now scored more PL goals for his current club than any other player!

Duvan Zapata

72

Club: *Atalanta* **DOB:** *1/4/91*

Country: *Colombia*

2018-19 was a big season for Duvan Zapata. After joining Atalanta on loan, he fired the Italian side to the Champions League for the first time in their history with 23 goals, outscoring Serie A superstars like Cristiano Ronaldo and Mauro Icardi in the process!

Nabil Fekir

71 🏴 🇫🇷

Club: *Real Betis* **DOB:** *18/7/93*
Country: *France*

Fekir is a goal threat because he's got so much talent! The playmaker ties defenders in knots with his quick feet and amazing flair, and his left foot is absolutely lethal – whether he's picking out a pass, curling in a cross or smashing a rocket strike into the top corner!

Mario Mandzukic

70 🏴 🇭🇷

Club: *Juventus* **DOB:** *21/5/86*
Country: *Croatia*

With goals in Germany, Spain and Italy, plus the Champions League, Mandzukic is an elite level striker. The Juve forward retired from international duty after the 2018 World Cup as Croatia's second top scorer of all time with 33 goals in 89 appearances. What a legend!

Billy Sharp

Wayne Rooney

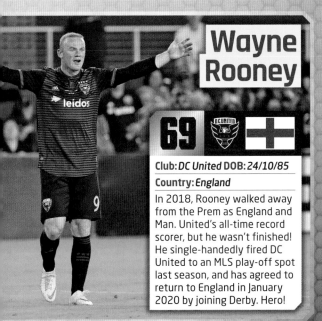

69 🏴 🏴󠁧󠁢󠁥󠁮󠁧󠁿

Club: *DC United* **DOB:** *24/10/85*
Country: *England*

In 2018, Rooney walked away from the Prem as England and Man. United's all-time record scorer, but he wasn't finished! He single-handedly fired DC United to an MLS play-off spot last season, and has agreed to return to England in January 2020 by joining Derby. Hero!

68 🏴 🏴󠁧󠁢󠁥󠁮󠁧󠁿

Club: *Sheff. United* **DOB:** *5/2/86*
Country: *England*

Sharp's been a Blades legend ever since his goals took them back up to the Championship in 2016-17 but, in January 2019, he became a Football League legend too! His 220th league goal made Sharp the highest goalscorer in the EFL during the 21st century. Wow!

STAT ATTACK!

164

Man. City hero Sergio Aguero moved up to sixth in the Premier League's all-time top scorers list by bagging his 164th goal in 2018-19!

7.69

Shane Long's strike for Southampton against Watford in April 2019 was the fastest goal in Premier League history!

40

Claudio Pizarro became the Bundesliga's oldest ever goalscorer when he netted for Werder Bremen at the age of 40 years and 227 days!

11

Man. City legend Aguero also matched a record set by Alan Shearer by bagging his 11th Prem hat-trick in 2018-19!

3

Souleymane Camara scored three Ligue 1 goals for Montpellier in 2018-19 without starting a game!

66

Neymar, Edinson Cavani and Kylian Mbappe were the deadliest trio in 2018-19 – they hit 66 league goals between them for PSG, one ahead of Barcelona's Lionel Messi, Luis Suarez and Ousmane Dembele!

11

Sampdoria star Fabio Quagliarella became the first player to score in 11 Serie A games in a row since Fiorentina's Gabriel Batistuta in 1994. Epic!

416

At the end of the 2018-19 season, Cristiano Ronaldo had scored more goals in Europe's top five leagues than any other player ever!

30

Kylian Mbappe and Lionel Messi were the only two players in Europe's top five leagues to score over 30 goals in 2018-19. Heroes!

12

The deadliest combo in Europe's top five leagues was Bournemouth's Ryan Fraser and Callum Wilson, who set each other up for 12 Prem goals in total!

61

Dortmund's Paco Alcacer averaged a goal every 61 minutes in the 2018-19 Bundesliga season – replacing ex-Wolfsburg forward Grafite as the deadliest finisher in the league's history!

Alexis Sanchez

67

Club: *Inter* **DOB:** *19/12/88*
Country: *Chile*

Chile's all-time top scorer has spent most of his career as a left winger that cuts inside to shoot, and his right foot is lethal! In his first ten seasons in Europe, Alexis scored over 120 goals in Italy, Spain and England, and almost 90 of them were with his right peg!

Joao Felix

65

Club: *Atletico Madrid*
Country: *Portugal* **DOB:** *10/11/99*

Joao Felix's debut season for Portuguese champs Benfica in 2018-19 was electric – he hit 20 goals in all comps, including a Europa League hat-trick! That put Europe's top clubs on red alert, and it was Atletico who moved first, signing him for an astonishing £113 million!

Josef Martinez

66

Club: *Atlanta Utd* **DOB:** *19/5/93*
Country: *Venezuela*

Ever since Martinez left Torino and arrived in MLS in 2017, he's absolutely dominated. Within two seasons he bagged 50 goals in just 54 games, and became the first player in the league's history to score over 30 goals in a single season!

Lucas Moura

64

Club: *Tottenham* **DOB:** *13/8/92*
Country: *Brazil*

Samba star Lucas fired himself up the rankings of our list with one of the most dramatic hat-tricks ever! His three goals in Spurs' incredible comeback against Ajax in last season's Champions League semi-final will go down in history – and took him to 95 career goals!

Marko Arnautovic

63

Club: *Shanghai SIPG*

Country: *Austria* **DOB:** *19/4/89*

Arnautovic has always been a player with tons of talent, but he found his best form at West Ham. The forward combines pace and power with a top-class touch and awesome skills, and those abilities didn't go unnoticed – he a sealed a £22.4 million move to China last summer!

Diego Costa

62

Club: *Atletico Madrid*

Country: *Spain* **DOB:** *7/10/88*

Between 2012 and 2017, Costa was one of the world's deadliest strikers with 115 goals for Atletico and Chelsea. He's not been quite as prolific recently, but his power and aggression still make him a nightmare for defenders!

Lorenzo Insigne

61

Club: *Napoli* **DOB:** *4/6/91*

Country: *Italy*

Napoli have become one of Italy's best teams over the last few years, and Insigne's been right at the heart of it. Since he first broke into the team in 2012-13, they've only finished outside of Serie A's top three once, and the winger has been key to that with 58 goals!

Carlos Vela

60

Club: *Los Angeles FC*

Country: *Mexico* **DOB:** *1/3/89*

2018 was a good year for the ex-Arsenal forward with 14 MLS goals for Los Angeles FC, but 2019 has been even better – Vela's scored over 20 league goals for the first time in his career! He's been absolutely destroying opponents with his wand of a left foot all year!

Richarlison

59

Club: *Everton* **DOB:** *10/5/97*

Country: *Brazil*

Eyebrows were raised when Everton spent £35 million on Richarlison in 2018, but he silenced his critics with 14 goals in his first season. The young forward has proved himself on the international stage too, with six goals in his first 13 games for Brazil!

Teemu Pukki

58

Club: *Norwich* **DOB:** *29/3/90*

Country: *Finland*

Pukki might be one of the best free transfers of all time! The ex-Celtic striker joined Norwich from Brondby in 2018 and bossed the Championship. Only one striker has scored more goals in a single Championship season than the 29 he bagged for The Canaries in 2018-19!

Raul Jimenez

56

Club: *Wolves* **DOB:** *5/5/91*

Country: *Mexico*

Wolves signed Jimenez on loan at the start of 2018-19 and they didn't even wait until the end of the season before spending £30 million to make it permanent! With 17 goals in all competitions, the Mexico striker had the best European campaign of his career so far!

Hirving Lozano

55

Club: *Napoli* **DOB:** *30/7/95*

Country: *Mexico*

Only one player scored more goals in the last two Eredivisie seasons combined than Lozano – the wicked winger netted 17 in each campaign and got eight assists in both too! That led to Napoli paying £39 million for him last summer, a record fee for a Mexican player. Wow!

Alfredo Morelos

57

Club: *Rangers* **DOB:** *21/6/96*

Country: *Colombia*

Rangers took a gamble when they plucked Morelos from HJK after scoring 11 goals in 12 games for the Finnish side, but it's definitely paid off. He scored 14 goals in his debut campaign, then bagged last season's Scottish Prem Golden Boot with 18 net-busters!

Moussa Dembele

54

Club: *Lyon* **DOB:** *12/7/96*

Country: *France*

Dembele was only 19 when he bagged 15 Championship goals for Fulham in 2015-16, and then he buried another 51 in all comps for Celtic in just two years! After 20 goals in his first season for Lyon, the huge French talent is showing no signs of slowing down!

Florian Thauvin

53

Club: *Marseille* **DOB:** *26/1/93*
Country: *France*

Thauvin flopped at Newcastle, but since leaving he's shown why the club thought he was worth £15 million in 2015. The winger uses his pace and trickery to get into goalscoring positions, and has rattled in more than 50 Ligue 1 goals since re-joining Marseille!

Moussa Marega

52

Club: *Porto* **DOB:** *14/4/91*
Country: *Mali*

Marega has been one of the deadliest forwards in Portugal over the last few seasons, but he really proved why he's a top-class goal machine in the 2018-19 Champions League. He bagged six goals in total, and Porto won every single match that he scored in!

Andrej Kramaric

51

Club: *Hoffenheim* **DOB:** *19/6/91*
Country: *Croatia*

Andrej only joined Hoffenheim in 2015, but he's already hit 50 Bundesliga goals for them and become their all-time record scorer in the competition! It's no surprise he bags so many – only Robert Lewandowski has taken more Bundesliga shots in the last three seasons!

Arkadiusz Milik

50

Club: *Napoli* **DOB:** *28/2/94*
Country: *Poland*

Napoli signed Milik from Ajax for £28 million in 2016, but injuries totally ruined his first two seasons in Italy – he only started seven Serie A games. But once he stayed fit, he hit top form! In 2018-19, he got 20 goals in all competitions – and there's more to come!

Luuk de Jong

49

Club: *Sevilla* **DOB:** *27/8/90*

Country: *Netherlands*

Since he made his debut for De Graafschap back in 2008, de Jong has scored over 130 Eredivisie goals! 28 of those came last season for PSV as he finished as the division's top scorer, and that led to Sevilla paying £13.5 million to snap him up last summer!

Memphis Depay

48

Club: *Lyon* **DOB:** *13/2/94*

Country: *Netherlands*

Depay is another dangerous Dutchman and he can score any type of goal! Memphis has the dribbling ability to create chances for himself, the pace to run behind the defence and a wicked right foot to shoot from anywhere! Plus, he's a world-class free-kick taker!

Callum Wilson

47

Club: *Bournemouth* **DOB:** *27/2/92*

Country: *England*

Wilson is an absolute penalty-box poacher! Since the striker joined Bournemouth in 2014, only one of his 53 league goals have come from outside the area, while his first England goal on his international debut was a close-range tap-in too. He's just got lethal instincts!

FOOTY MIS-MATCH

Take a look at these pics of Kylian Mbappe busting net, then spot the ten differences!

WORDSEARCH

Find the Prem's all-time top 30 goalscorers in this mega grid!

```
    L M H J                                                           E X U O
    N G H O                                                           K L R W
    F K A A                                                           J N I C
    V Z S B                                                           T R H Y
    Q F S N                                                           F J X X
    D N E V                                                           E K G Z

B C L J P Y T P C W H S G T H W M X L B F K W R G R F H M
B L B A L B D O G P H G F S B E D E P S H S G O G Y D S P R
K T A I Y O T J M G Z E I N D A G S W U E C Y Z N H I L A S
E M I Z O K J L C L U E W U B F M A V E S H K F R E N E A H
A G N S U Y Q U S X G O K G H K V Q P A K O Z Q F N A T H E
N M K Z H R D N W K E J O B R S A W P R E L Q E X R N I J A
E E V J W E U L P K Y R U R I W Q R A X Y E U U B Y D S M R
L E T B U T R Z H J D F K K I Q A M W W M S R B M N A S K E
P V S L G B B I K Y G E A F U Y M O G G R V E A V H N I R R
V G N I U V C U N E O L I D L Y L A N E L K A D Y Z K E R E
U O P P X K K M H G H N T R N Z U E K L G H F X Y K O R U O
C H U H E E G K B Y H P R H R V K W S W W W V T X R R F R S L
A X T I B D H S T D O A E D A N A Q R S O G E E U U C E R S
C Y J Y R H H G R O V M M T N U K U Q M I A V T D Z O A O T
B H O Z Y O R K E P C G T L W L U O H I M H O A Y I C L O V
J I D G U S Y I C S S G X X M Z T Q J A D I C H H N Q T N A
L B I S C O L J Z O A H U O Y Q A R R Y Z U O L D B M C E D
T I A F R P J D C B I F Z W S W R Y L P X Y L I W X T W Y X
Y B S P O Z L O O L O O R B J Q R C A I O F G V Y S Y B K Q
D P T B U B U N L R E O L N K S M R C V W O U A F C X O U D
I E V M C D I Z E I Y B E M G F L V F I E H E N D Z F Y I O
C L L T H L Q U X A L W R G O I O S F G N V N N D E J C C H
B K Y H B W G X B W N E I F V E Z I Q V A U M I N H F P W O
G Q J U H A R E C W L G G N M R Q F Q D C W H S W K J O P S
L E D N L L D X D W K P D N W G U M F U W F L T V K M E E Y
A Y R Z D A M G O C O C U H R S L G J T S E L E X H R J E R
P M A R D V X F Z V I D J T I F A R L L Q E M L V L T N K F
O Z H Q A V T D V G M G Y G G T M S T K F A D R S F F N W
K L E I O R L K J J K S S Y H X P L N Z F R S O R F U N K H
P T I P G F D N R A A E H M T W A Y L L B W W O W M Z D V B
O P X K Y W V A N P E R S I E L R L N F Z T K Y M P M E J R
A E Y A D Z P G J R V W B G F U D M R U U Q J D Y D F J O V
I H L N F O E V B U G Q A S Y A Y L Q I N L D L Q B E N T B
P X B E J S Y S H L A V T I A O R A M D D F U P C T Y I G H
```

Adebayor	Defoe	Giggs	Lampard	Shearer
Aguero	Drogba	Hasselbaink	Le Tissier	Sheringham
Anelka	Dublin	Henry	Lukaku	Van Nistelrooy
Bent	Ferdinand	Heskey	Owen	Van Persie
Cole	Fowler	Kane	Rooney	Wright
Crouch	Gerrard	Keane	Scholes	Yorke

ANSWER ON PAGE

Mbaye Diagne

46

Club: *Club Brugge* **DOB:** *28/10/91*
Country: *Senegal*

Diagne was so good in a year at Kasimpasa, with 32 goals in just 34 league games, that Galatasaray snapped him up for a record transfer between Turkish clubs! The star added another ten goals in 12 games for the Super Lig champions, before joining Brugge on loan!

Olivier Giroud

45

Club: *Chelsea* **DOB:** *30/9/86*
Country: *France*

Fresh from winning the 2018 World Cup with France, Giroud fired Chelsea to a major trophy in 2019 too! He was the Europa League's top goalscorer with 11 strikes, including one in the final - no Frenchman has ever scored more goals in a single European campaign. Hero!

Bas Dost

44

Club: *E. Frankfurt* **DOB:** *31/5/89*
Country: *Netherlands*

Before joining Frankfurt, Dost had scored 20 or more goals in all comps on five occasions! He's won two Golden Boots in his career - once for Dutch club Heerenveen in 2011-12, and also for previous side Sporting in 2016-17, smashing home 34 goals in just 31 games!

Andrea Belotti

43

Club: *Torino* **DOB:** *20/12/93*
Country: *Italy*

Juventus might be top dogs in Turin, but none of their stars have scored as many Serie A goals as Torino's No.9 in the last four seasons! Belotti is a proper centre forward - he uses his power to lead the line for his team and is super clinical!

42

Club: *Galatasaray* **DOB:** *10/2/86*

Country: *Colombia*

'El Tigre' might be getting on a bit, but he's still preying on defenders and gobbling up chances! Not only is Falcao Colombia's all-time top scorer, the striker is also one of the most prolific players in Europa League history with 31 goals in just 33 games. Deadly!

Radamel Falcao

Marcus Rashford

41

Club: *Man. United* **DOB:** *31/10/97*

Country: *England*

We knew Rash would be a goal king when he scored four times in his first two pro games! The young gun's hit double figures in his last three campaigns for The Red Devils and, with his lightning pace, skill and rocket right foot, he'll get loads more!

Luka Jovic

40

Club: *Real Madrid* **DOB:** *23/12/97*
Country: *Serbia*

Jovic has been destined for the top ever since he became Red Star Belgrade's youngest ever goalscorer at the age of 16! In 2019, he earned a £62 million move to Real after scoring 17 Bundesliga goals for Frankfurt, plus another ten on the road to the Europa League semis!

Paulo Dybala

39

Club: *Juventus* **DOB:** *15/11/93*
Country: *Argentina*

Argentina and Juventus star Dybala has an absolute wand of a left foot! Whether he's using it to dribble through tackles, whip in crosses or link attacks, it's a serious weapon and proper deadly in front of goal – he's used it to bury more than 90% of his Serie A goals!

Zlatan Ibrahimovic

38

Club: *LA Galaxy* **DOB:** *3/10/81*
Country: *Sweden*

It takes a really special player to score so many goals in so many different countries, and that's exactly what Zlatan is. He's terrorised defenders in Sweden, Italy, Spain, France, England, Netherlands and USA, while also bagging 62 goals in international football too!

Marco Reus

37

Club: *Borussia Dortmund*
Country: *Germany* **DOB:** *31/5/89*

Dortmund's Reus isn't even a striker, yet he's still one of the most dangerous goalscorers in Germany. The Borussia skipper is a master at timing his runs into the box to get on the end of crosses and, when the ball drops at his feet, he hardly ever misses!

Gonzalo Higuain

36 JUVENTUS

Club: *Juventus* **DOB:** *10/12/87*
Country: *Argentina*

Italy's Serie A has seen some incredible strikers over the years, but none of them have ever scored as many goals in a single season as Higuain's 36 net-busters for Napoli in 2015-16! Since he arrived in Italy in 2013, nobody's scored more goals in the league!

Gareth Bale

35

Club: *Real Madrid* **DOB:** *16/7/89*
Country: *Wales*

Bale's scored over 100 goals for Real, including some of the club's most important goals of the last decade! The Welsh wizard bagged an incredible winner in the 2014 Copa del Rey final and was on target in two CL finals – including an amazing bicycle-kick in 2018!

Gabriel Jesus

34 MANCHESTER CITY

Club: *Man. City* **DOB:** *3/4/97*
Country: *Brazil*

Jesus has proven himself as a world-class forward for both Brazil and City, so it's easy to forget that he's still in his early 20s. His demon dribbling, epic pace and movement give him the ability to get into brilliant positions, and that's why he's such a total goal machine!

STAT ATTACK!

238

Cristiano Ronaldo and Lionel Messi have scored 238 CL goals between them – that's almost as many as the next four top goalscorers put together!

24

After five CL goals in 2018-19, Harry Kane is now Tottenham's all-time leading goalscorer in European footy!

11

Olivier Giroud's 11 Europa League goals for Chelsea in 2018-19 was the best performance ever by a French player in a single European season!

34

Cristiano Ronaldo became the oldest scorer of a CL hat-trick when he banged in three goals against Atletico Madrid in 2019 at the age of 34 years and 35 days!

50

Bayern Munich striker Robert Lewandowski became only the seventh player to score 50 career Champions League goals in 2018-19!

6

No player has scored more CL goals at the Johan Cruyff Arena than Cristiano Ronaldo – even though he's never played for Ajax!

19

Joao Felix became the youngest player to score a Europa League hat-trick when he bagged an epic treble for Benfica against Eintracht Frankfurt in 2019!

65

As well as extending his record-breaking Champions League tally to 126, Cristiano Ronaldo bagged his 65th goal in the knockout stages in 2018-19 – more than anyone!

12

Son Heung-min became the highest-scoring Asian player in Champions League history by bagging his 12th goal in the competition against Man. City!

5

By scoring against Arsenal in the 2019 Europa League final, Pedro became the fifth player in history to score in both the Champions League and Europa League finals!

3

Liverpool's Divock Origi had three shots in eight CL games in 2018-19, but they all went in – against Barça in the semi-final and Tottenham in the final. Wow!

Wissam Ben Yedder

33

Club: *Monaco* **DOB:** *12/8/90*

Country: *France*

Sevilla splashed out on Ben Yedder to replace top scorer Kevin Gameiro in 2016, and the France ace was an amazing signing for the Spanish side. He topped the club's scoring charts every single season, before returning to France with Monaco last summer!

Timo Werner

32

Club: *RB Leipzig* **DOB:** *6/3/96*

Country: *Germany*

Germany have been hunting a world-class striker ever since record goalscorer Miroslav Klose retired in 2014 – and Werner might be the man. The young striker uses his electric pace to run behind defences, and already has more than 60 Bundesliga goals to his name!

Iago Aspas

31

Club: *Celta Vigo* **DOB:** *1/8/87*

Country: *Spain*

Aspas isn't just Celta Vigo's top goalscorer, he's the most important player they've ever had! In two spells, he's scored more goals than anyone else and delivers when they need him most. He single-handedly saved them from relegation in 2018-19 with 20 goals!

Jamie Vardy

30

Club: *Leicester* **DOB:** *11/1/87*
Country: *England*

Vardy sealed his status as a Leicester legend in 2015-16 when he fired the club to the Premier League title! He's not stopped scoring since then either, and last season became the first Foxes player to score 100 goals for the club since Gary Lineker in the 1980s!

Edin Dzeko

29

Club: *Roma* **DOB:** *17/3/86*
Country: *Bosnia & Herzegovina*

Bosnia's all-time record scorer has won Golden Boots in the Bundesliga, Serie A and Europa League during his top career, while also grabbing another 50 goals in the Prem! He's got bags of power and is a deadly finisher with either foot!

Paco Alcacer

27

Club: *Borussia Dortmund*
Country: *Spain* **DOB:** *30/8/93*

Paco began 2018-19 on fire, scoring nine goals in just six games for club and country, and he didn't slow down! The ex-Barcelona superstar went on to score 18 times in the Bundesliga, averaging a goal every 61 minutes - the best record in the league's history!

Alexandre Lacazette

28

Club: *Arsenal* **DOB:** *28/5/91*
Country: *France*

Arsenal broke their transfer record to sign Lacazette in 2017 after the France striker smashed 91 goals in just three seasons for Lyon! He's carried on that form in England, too - grabbing double figures for goals in each of his first two seasons with The Gunners!

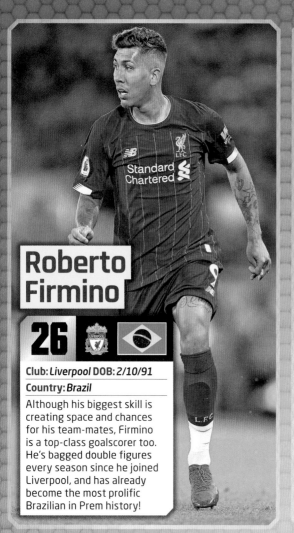

Roberto Firmino

26

Club: Liverpool **DOB:** 2/10/91
Country: Brazil

Although his biggest skill is creating space and chances for his team-mates, Firmino is a top-class goalscorer too. He's bagged double figures every season since he joined Liverpool, and has already become the most prolific Brazilian in Prem history!

Romelu Lukaku

25

Club: Inter **DOB:** 13/5/93
Country: Belgium

When he was in Anderlecht's youth team, the Inter new boy hit a phenomenal 121 goals in 68 matches, so he was always going to be a goal machine! He bagged over 100 Prem goals, but he's saved his best form for Belgium – nobody's scored more for The Red Devils!

Son Heung-min

24

Club: Tottenham **DOB:** 8/7/92
Country: South Korea

In the last few seasons, Son has gone from a hard-working squad player to one of the most dangerous attackers in the Prem. He's totally two-footed, has tons of pace and energy, and no Asian player has scored more goals in CL history!

Dries Mertens

23 N

Club: *Napoli* **DOB:** *6/5/87*

Country: *Belgium*

Switching Mertens from a winger to a No.9 was a stroke of genius from ex-Napoli boss Maurizio Sarri. The Belgium star can use his speed and trickery to tie centre-backs in knots, and he's got his sights on Marek Hamsik's all-time scoring record for the club!

Eden Hazard

22

Club: *Real Madrid* **DOB:** *7/1/91*

Country: *Belgium*

Hazard's insane dribbling is what makes him such a goal threat. Whenever the winger picks up the ball within sight of goal, defenders know that he's capable of taking it past them and slotting it home with ease - that's how he got most of his 85 Prem goals!

Dusan Tadic

21

Club: *Ajax* **DOB:** *20/11/88*

Country: *Serbia*

Joining Ajax has to be the best decision of Tadic's career! The forward had a phenomenal season, with 38 goals in total as Ajax won a domestic double! He also scored in a famous 4-1 victory over Real Madrid at the Bernabeu, as his side went all the way to the CL semi-finals!

Ciro Immobile

20

Club: *Lazio* **DOB:** *20/2/90*

Country: *Italy*

Before joining Lazio, Immobile had played for eight different teams, but he's found his home with the Roman club. Since he joined them, nobody's scored more times in Serie A and, in 2017-18, he broke a 40-year club record by scoring 41 goals in all competitions. Superstar!

Nicolas Pepe

19

Club: *Arsenal* **DOB:** *29/5/95*

Country: *Cote d'Ivoire*

Pepe's left foot might just be one of the most dangerous in Europe right now – he used it to score all but one of his 22 Ligue 1 goals in 2018-19! His form for Lille put Europe on red-alert and Arsenal won the race to sign him, splashing out a club record £72 million!

Mauro Icardi

18

Club: *PSG* **DOB:** *19/2/93*
Country: *Argentina*

Barça are kicking themselves for letting Icardi leave at the age of 18! The Argentina ace has been prolific with over 100 goals in six seasons at Inter, and now he's totally bossing it at PSG! He has the ability to finish from anywhere with either foot or his head!

Krzysztof Piatek

17

Club: *AC Milan* **DOB:** *1/7/95*
Country: *Poland*

Half the clubs in Europe were chasing striker Piatek when he became the first player of the 2018-19 season to score ten league goals. Milan won the race to sign him, and within five matches he'd become the quickest player in their history to score six goals in all comps!

Fabio Quagliarella

16

Club: *Sampdoria* **DOB:** *31/1/83*
Country: *Italy*

The veteran striker is known for scoring spectacular goals, but since joining Samp he's been unstoppable. No current star has scored more Serie A goals than Fabio and, after bagging a career high 26 at the age of 36, it doesn't look like he'll be caught soon!

STAT ATTACK!

7

England's all-time top scorer in the competition is Alan Shearer, who scored seven goals in nine matches and bagged the Golden Boot at Euro '96!

23

Republic Of Ireland hero Robbie Keane scored 23 goals in Euro qualifying – more than any other player in history!

4

Zinedine Zidane holds the joint-record for penalties scored at Euro finals alongside Shearer. They both scored two in normal play and another two in shootouts!

29

Cristiano Ronaldo holds the outright record for goals at finals and in qualifying with 29 in total, and is the only player to score in four different tournaments!

2000

Euro 2000 was the only final ever to be won by a Golden Goal. France's David Trezeguet slammed in the winner after 103 minutes against unlucky Italy!

4

Germany are the only country to produce four Golden Boot winners. Gerd Muller, Dieter Muller, Klaus Allofs and Karl-Heinz Riedle all won the famous award!

1984

At Euro '84 in France, Les Bleus legend Michel Platini scored nine goals in five matches, including TWO hat-tricks – nobody else has scored more than one in Euros history!

32

Antoine Griezmann bagged the Golden Boot in 2016 by scoring six goals – the best performance by any player since Platini's record 32 years earlier!

9

Cristiano Ronaldo and Michel Platini are the joint-top scorers in Euros history with nine goals each. CR7 took 21 games to reach that tally, while the France legend did it in just five!

6

Eder became only the sixth substitute to score in a Euros final when he netted Portugal's winner against France in 2016!

18

In 2004, Switzerland striker Johan Vonlanthen became the youngest goalscorer in the competition's history by bagging against France!

Karim Benzema

15

Club: *Real Madrid* **DOB:** *19/12/87*

Country: *France*

If Karim had played in another era, he'd be an absolute legend! His time in La Liga has been overshadowed by Ronaldo and Messi, yet only the legendary duo have outscored him since he arrived! He's sixth in Real's all-time charts, while only four stars have hit more CL goals!

Sadio Mane

14

Club: *Liverpool* **DOB:** *10/4/92*

Country: *Senegal*

After scoring ten goals on the road to the 2018 CL final, including one in the final itself, Mane became even more of a goal king in 2019, sharing the Prem Golden Boot with team-mate Mo Salah and helping The Reds win the Champo League!

Antoine Griezmann

13

Club: *Barcelona* **DOB:** *21/3/91*

Country: *France*

Griezmann has been seriously unlucky to miss out on a Ballon d'Or in the last few years. His goals won Euro 2016's Golden Boot, took Atletico to a Europa League trophy and fired France to World Cup glory! Can Grizi finally win it at Barcelona?

Raheem Sterling

12 | Manchester City | ✚

Club: *Man. City* **DOB:** *8/12/94*

Country: *England*

Sterling burst onto the scene as an electric winger that ran at defenders, but under Pep Guardiola he's become a clinical goalscorer! A lot of his 17 Prem goals in 2018-19 seemed like tap-ins, but that's because his movement is just so good!

Pierre-Emerick Aubameyang

11 | Arsenal

Club: *Arsenal* **DOB:** *18/6/89*

Country: *Gabon*

Auba was the third player to share the 2019 Prem Golden Boot with Salah and Mane – not bad for a player in his first full Prem season! The Arsenal hitman uses his pace to run in behind defences and, when he gets in on goal, he's ruthless!

Neymar

10

Club: *PSG* **DOB:** *5/2/92*
Country: *Brazil*

Neymar has tons of tricks, but he's also a lethal goalscorer! Since arriving in Europe back in 2013, he's scored more than 150 goals for Barcelona and PSG, become the most prolific Brazilian in CL history and is closing in on Pele's all-time scoring record for Brazil too!

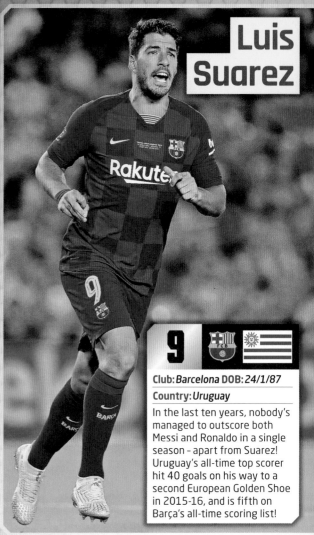

Luis Suarez

9

Club: *Barcelona* **DOB:** *24/1/87*
Country: *Uruguay*

In the last ten years, nobody's managed to outscore both Messi and Ronaldo in a single season – apart from Suarez! Uruguay's all-time top scorer hit 40 goals on his way to a second European Golden Shoe in 2015-16, and is fifth on Barça's all-time scoring list!

Edinson Cavani

8

Club: *PSG* **DOB:** *14/2/87*
Country: *Uruguay*

PSG smashed their transfer record to buy Cavani after the ex-Napoli striker bagged the Serie A Golden Boot with 29 goals in 2012-13. He's picked up two more top scorer awards in Ligue 1 and broke Zlatan Ibrahimovic's all-time scoring record for the club in 2018!

Harry Kane

7 Tottenham Hotspur · England

Club: *Tottenham* **DOB:** *28/7/93*

Country: *England*

Kane has records on his mind! He's already Spurs' top Prem scorer and he's not far off their all-time record! The World Cup Golden Boot winner raced into England's top 20 scorers too, and has his sights set big time on Wayne Rooney's top spot!

Mohamed Salah

6 Liverpool · Egypt

Club: *Liverpool* **DOB:** *15/6/92*

Country: *Egypt*

Some people thought Salah might be a one-season wonder after 44 goals for The Reds in 2017-18, but he's proven those doubters wrong! The Egyptian followed up his sizzling debut season by bagging another Prem Golden Boot and netting in the Champo League final!

FACE IN THE CROWD

Ten of the Prem's top scorers from 2018-19 are hiding in this crazy crowd... find them!

Paul Pogba

Glenn Murray

Pierre-Emerick Aubameyang

Sadio Mane

Raheem Sterling

Callum Wilson

Richarlison

Raul Jimenez

Jamie Vardy

Harry Kane

GOAL MACHINES BRAIN-BUSTER

Can you score ten out of ten in our goal machines quiz?

1. Sadio Mane, Mohamed Salah and which other striker was joint-top Prem goalscorer in 2018-19?

2. How many goals did Lionel Messi score on his way to winning the 2018-19 CL Golden Boot?

3. True or False? MLS goal king Bradley Wright-Phillips is the son of legendary striker Ian Wright!

4. Chelsea broke their transfer record to sign which Spain striker from Real Madrid in 2017?

5. James Norwood was the top goalscorer in which English league in 2018-19 – League One or Two?

6. Which Spanish club did lethal Argentina striker Mauro Icardi play for during his youth career?

7. Which Premier League legend is the Netherlands' all-time top goalscorer?

8. All-time MLS top scorer Chris Wondolowski played international football for which country?

9. Which Portugal forward is the joint-top goalscorer in European Championship history?

10. Who did Gylfi Sigurdsson overtake as Iceland's all-time top Premier League goalscorer?

1 ....
2 ....
3 ....
4 ....
5 ....
6 ....
7 ....
8 ....
9 ....
10 ....

ANSWERS ON PAGE

Sergio Aguero

5

Club: *Man. City* **DOB:** *2/6/88*

Country: *Argentina*

Take a look at some of the records Aguero has broken in his Prem career. Nobody's got more hat-tricks – 11, nobody's scored more times in a single game – five, and only one other forward has scored 20 goals or more in five consecutive seasons! City's all-time top scorer will carry on banging in goals and breaking records!

DID YOU KNOW?

Aguero has the best goals-to-game ratio of any footballer with 100 career Premier League goals!

Robert Lewandowski

4

Club: *Bayern Munich*

Country: *Poland* **DOB:** *21/8/88*

Whether he's wearing a Bayern shirt or a Poland one, Lewa is absolutely deadly in front of goal! Last season he collected his fourth Bundesliga Golden Boot, and has hit more goals in the German league than any foreign player! He also holds the all-time records for goals in European qualifying for both World Cups and Euros. Ledge!

DID YOU KNOW?

Last season, only Lionel Messi scored more Champo League goals than Lewa, who also became the seventh player in history to score 50 CL goals!

Kylian Mbappe

3

Club: *PSG* **DOB:** *20/12/98*
Country: *France*

If any player has a chance of replacing Lionel Messi as the best player on the planet, it's Mbappe. He's already won more trophies and scored more goals than the Barcelona legend had at the same age, and Leo was the only player to outscore the wonderkid in Europe's top five leagues last season! It's scary to think how good he will be in a few years' time!

DID YOU KNOW?

In 2018, Mbappe became the youngest player to score in a World Cup Final since Brazil icon Pele in 1958. Wow!

Cristiano Ronaldo

2

Club: *Juventus* **DOB:** *5/2/85*

Country: *Portugal*

Ronaldo is one of the greatest players of all time because he's scored goals everywhere! Not many forwards have been prolific in England, Spain and Italy, plus he's also the record scorer in Champions League history! On top of that, the Portugal legend is closing in on Ali Daei's all-time goal record in international footy too!

DID YOU KNOW?

Ronaldo's hat-trick against Switzerland in last summer's UEFA Nations League was the 53rd treble of his career!

Lionel Messi

1

Club: *Barcelona* **DOB:** *24/6/87*

Country: *Argentina*

Who else could top MATCH's countdown of the planet's most lethal goal machines? 2019 was an incredible year for Messi – he won Golden Boots in La Liga and the Champions League, as well as the European Golden Shoe for the sixth time! The scary thing is, it was far from his best campaign – he's had five more prolific seasons!

Messi holds the world record for most goals ever in a single calendar year. In 2012, he scored 91 times for club and country!

STAT ATTACK!

LIONEL MESSI

MESSI tops our list once again! Check out his incredible numbers from the 2018-19 season...

6

Messi won the Pichichi Trophy by finishing as La Liga's top goalscorer for a record sixth time!

51

Barça's all-time top scorer bagged 51 goals in 50 games in all competitions – the sixth time he's reached that tally during his awesome career!

His stunning free-kick v Liverpool was his 26th Champions League goal against English clubs in just 34 games – no player has hit more goals against teams from one country!

26

33

In March he scored his 33rd La Liga hat-trick – only Cristiano Ronaldo has scored more!

10

Messi's goals fired Barça to the league title – the tenth of his career!

Leo's strike against Liverpool was also his 600th Barcelona goal – exactly 14 years after his very first one for the club v Albacete in May 2005!

600

14 — Messi's one of only three players to have scored in 14 Champions League seasons in a row!

419 — He became the first player to score 400 La Liga goals, ending the season with 419 in total, and extending his lead over Cristiano Ronaldo at the top of the all-time charts to over 100!

3 — He bagged his third European Golden Shoe in a row and his sixth in total – another all-time record!

8 — Eight of his goals in 2018-19 came from free-kicks – more than any player in Europe's top five leagues!

66 — He holds the record for most goals in the Champions League group stage after bagging six in 2018-19!

12 — Messi scored 12 Champions League goals last season to win the top scorer award for the first time since 2015 – ending CR7's three-year dominance!

MESSI

DRAW YOUR FAVE GOAL MACHINE!

You've seen our top 100 goal machines, now pick your fave and draw them on the opposite page for the chance to win a prize!

Name:

Date of birth:

Address:

Mobile:

Email:

Face In The Crowd P48

Wordsearch P29

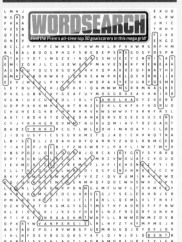

Find the Prem's all-time top 30 goalscorers in this mega grid!

Brain-Buster P49

1. Pierre-E. Aubameyang
2. 12
3. True
4. Alvaro Morata
5. League Two
6. Barcelona
7. Robin van Persie
8. USA
9. Cristiano Ronaldo
10. Eidur Gudjohnsen

Footy Mis-Match P28

LOVE MATCH?
GET IT DELIVERED EVERY WEEK!

FREE 16-PAGE POSTER PULLOUT FOR YOUR WALL!

15 POSTERS

BURNLEY CHELSEA C.PALACE EVERTON MAN UNITED NEWCASTLE TOTTENHAM WATFORD WEST HAM

MATCH!

GOLDEN BOOT BATTLE!

WHO WILL BE THE PREM'S TOP SCORER?

4 ISSUES FOR JUST £1!*

PACKED EVERY WEEK WITH...

★ Red-hot gear

★ FIFA tips

★ Stats & quizzes

★ Massive stars

★ Posters & pics

& loads more!